T0082888

Fly High: *A 30-Day Writing Journey to Shift from Worry to Peace*

SHERYL WALKER

authorHOUSE·

AuthorHouse™
1663 Liberty Drive
Bloomington, IN 47403
www.authorhouse.com
Phone: 833-262-8899

© *2021 Sheryl Walker. All rights reserved.*

No part of this book may be reproduced, stored in a retrieval system, or transmitted by any means without the written permission of the author.

Published by AuthorHouse 08/13/2021

ISBN: 978-1-6655-3400-0 (sc)
ISBN: 978-1-6655-3399-7 (e)

Library of Congress Control Number: 2021915935

Print information available on the last page.

Any people depicted in stock imagery provided by Getty Images are models, and such images are being used for illustrative purposes only. Certain stock imagery © Getty Images.

This book is printed on acid-free paper.

Because of the dynamic nature of the Internet, any web addresses or links contained in this book may have changed since publication and may no longer be valid. The views expressed in this work are solely those of the author and do not necessarily reflect the views of the publisher, and the publisher hereby disclaims any responsibility for them.

Scripture quotations marked NIV are taken from the Holy Bible, New International Version®. NIV®. Copyright © 1973, 1978, 1984 by International Bible Society. Used by permission of Zondervan. All rights reserved. [Biblica]

"Don't worry. You can relax."
– God

Where is your focus?
Where is your faith?

If I am burdened with worry,
I might not be praying enough
I might not be following the prompting of the Holy Spirit enough.
Am I paying attention?
Am I listening?
When you take things off your shoulders and give it to God,
Truly give it to God,
Your mind and perspective shifts.
God changes things
Once we truly surrender to him.

"Therefore I tell you, do not worry about your life, what you will eat or drink; or about your body, what you will wear. Is not life more than food, and the body more than clothes? Look at the birds of the air; they do not sow or reap or store away in barns, and yet your heavenly Father feeds them. Are you not much more valuable than they? Can any one of you by worrying add a single hour to your life?"

— Matthew 6:25–27 (New International Version)

Remember, God is EXTREMELY dependable, consistent, and unfailing.

How has God been reliable lately with the little things? What will God do for the big things?

One day at a time
One thing at a time
Do it scared
Tap into your inner strong self
Either you win or you learn
No failures here

INTRODUCTION

Birds begin each day on a quest to find food. As they flit about, they don't appear worried or frazzled in any way. They see another bird feasting and they join them. If unsuccessful, they move to another location. They seem to follow the prompting of the Holy Spirit to fulfill their daily sustenance. They have a constant reassurance and quiet confidence that they will be okay and that their needs will be fulfilled.

We all have worries. We worry about the world, our country, and our own personal stuff. Worry impacts almost everyone in some capacity. Some individuals have lived a very challenging life with devastations that are unfathomable. With every new battle we face, there may be new reasons to worry and feel anxious. Our degree of worry varies based on so many different and complex factors. Some of us have more of a predisposition or inclination to worry. Some of us live with worries that are a result of our past. For many of us, intense worry is our go-to response to stressful or uncomfortable situations.

Worry keeps us frozen and unable to live at the full capacity of life. We may feel hesitant about taking certain risks because if something doesn't go the way we planned, we would be to blame. At times, worrying can cause debilitating sorrow that makes us feel like we are drowning or close to a nervous breakdown. This can get in the way of us functioning at optimal levels.

Some problems or issues can't be solved in advance, so worrying often results in wasted time and energy. Worry is a thief. It takes our attention and focus. It steals our peace and productivity. It consumes our joy. Worry does not change the outcome. We waste a lot of time unnecessarily suffering and agonizing over hypothetical outcomes. It's like we are mice on a wheel running in circles, making no progress as we spin around and around. While a lot of worries seem justified, the reality is that most of our everyday worries are not worth getting worked up about. We tend to get sideswiped by other random stuff in life. Spinning wastes away our ability to live fully in the calling God has for our lives.

But why do we worry so much when God has told us time and time again to trust him and to cast all of our cares on him? God is the master supervisor. His detailed plan for our lives is so intricate and so amazing. How can we be more like the birds? Why do we continue to wrestle with trusting God? To trust God is to be free from worry. It is to have peace. Worry is the opposite of peace.

It's okay to be sad, disappointed, overwhelmed, among many other feelings and emotions. That's being human. Don't resist that feeling, but don't remain there. You can be cautious and concerned, but at the same time not spin and waste away your time, energy, and life. Accept whatever will be and trust God to turn all things around for your good.

For me, worry is an indicator that an area of my life needs focused prayer. When I'm in a constant state of worry, I'm usually too caught up in my feelings and not thinking rationally. Drawing nearer to God shows that we are serious about our relationship with him. When I'm worrying, I must bolster my faith and give the situation entirely to God. I need to move out of the way and let the true commander in chief lead the situation. I move, but only when God tells me to move. I have to listen for God's voice. I might need to remove myself from the stimulus that is causing any added agitation. I might need to have key conversations and speak my truth. I might have to engage in more self-care practices and ensure I am getting sufficient rest. I might have to make up my mind as to how I am going to operate in a situation. Maybe I have to free up my time and commit to less things. Maybe I have to commit more of my time to the things that matter. Maybe I need to ask for more support. I know I must make a move. When I feel less than optimistic, I might need to list out God's past faithfulness. No matter the key move, with prayer and intention, worries can subside.

As I wrote this book, I was in my own season of worry. This book was written during the COVID-19 pandemic, and when a series of senseless killings of Black people in the United States sparked protests and looting. The pandemic alone brought on major worry. And here we were again having to reckon with the sin of racism and white supremacy in America. To add to this, there was the US presidential election in the midst of it all. This was a season of worry overload. I devised and reflected on strategies as I worked through my own heightened worry. Considering the fact that life is filled with tense moments, how can we unlearn this coping habit, or at least check ourselves in the midst of it, and do a little bit less of it? Life is less enjoyable with excessive worry.

One thing I know for sure: worry is a fraud, worry is a liar, and worry will have you magnify and spin in misfortune, destroy your health, and forget past victories. God really does have you in the palm of his hands. Every single detail. He is our provider. God is the way, the truth, and the light. God is for you. God is so much greater than our circumstance.

When Do We Worry?

We can't blame COVID-19 alone for our worrying habit. Most of us were already expert worriers before the pandemic.

Let's focus on *when* we worry.

We often worry when there is:

1. Uncertainty
   - We question, "How will I survive?" or "Will everything be okay?"
   - There is a desire, but we don't see a clear path. We wonder how things will manifest. We don't know how things will play out. We dwell and ruminate about life's what-ifs.
   - We receive bad news.
   - There's instability in our circumstances—family, finances, career, health, relationships, future, etc.
   - It feels like everything is crashing into each other.

- Feeling inadequately prepared.
- There's a lack of information you feel you should know.
- When there is abuse—verbally, emotionally, mentally, and physically.
- A feeling of regret that we got ourselves into a situation and can't see our way out.
- Needing to put the love and care of our loved ones in someone else's hands.
- There's too much good or bad happening at once.
- We question whether we will be able to rebound after rejection.
- There's an overwhelming and endless to-do list.
- Trying something new and challenging.
- Feeling overwhelmed by a global pandemic.
- Feeling stress and burnout.
- Wondering how you will endure if the inevitable happens.
- Comparison, envy, jealousy—what about me?
- It's tail-spinning into the worst-case scenario.
- There are seasons of change.
- When we have to have a difficult conversation or address the elephant in the room.

2. High risk of loss
   - Pain, sickness, or ill health.
   - Layoffs and job insecurity, a risk of providing basic needs, providing adequately for child(ren), etc.
   - A loss of power.
   - Someone or something is taken that we feel we have earned or deserve.
   - A risk someone might abandon us.
   - When we know we have to change the dynamics of a close relationship.
   - A fear that others will forget about us.

3. Memories of the past that now serve as triggers
   - Identity triggers: Will we be accepted? Will we measure up?
   - Prolonged trauma.
   - A reminder of past (unhealed) wounds.
   - Strife within our family unit.
   - So many mistakes and missteps in our relationships—we wonder if certain individuals will ever forgive us. Tension lingers.
   - The possibility of going back to a negatively familiar situation. It might even be a downright dangerous situation. We know what to expect, but we are not waiting in anticipation for God to do something new.

4. Waiting
   - A waiting season. How will things turn out? How long will I have to wait?
   - A delay of something that is important to what we perceive to be our mark of success.
   - Wondering if there will be a breakthrough in our health, finances, etc.

5. Blame, shame, and regret
   - Concern others will perceive us as a failure or not meeting the standard.
   - Others will see us for how we perceive ourselves to be.
   - An obsession or shame over our past mistakes.
   - Wishing things could have been different.

Purpose

The purpose of this book is to give you a space to reflect, process, provide hope, and maybe reassurance or a reminder of who God is. I have created this 30-Day writing journey to help guide you on how to approach your worries and then work through them with various writing prompts. The goal is to try to reduce the unnecessary worry that is within your realm of control. You'll want to stop feeding your worries and searching for corroborating evidence. You'll want to shut the door to worry or leave the door slightly ajar.

The goal is to find something positive on the other side of this 30-Day writing journey. Make today the day you stop giving away your mental energy to thoughts that bear no fruit. Reduce your investment in uncertainty. Remain grounded in the certainty of who God is. Work to pull yourself out of the worry pit. Give it to God, and then rest.

The 30-Day Writing Journey to shift from worry to peace is a . . .

No-judgment zone. It is also a journey for us dwellers who are open to considering a new way of looking at things. There are differences between worry, fear, anxiety, and depression. The depth and complexity of those ailments will require professional assistance. I am an educator and one who believes individuals have the capacity to work through their problems with God and come out on the other side with some form of enlightenment. Will everything be resolved? Probably not. Can you move along the continuum to at least begin feeling better? Absolutely!

This writing journey frames the worry thought process to help you think and seek God through a new lens. This journey might shift your thinking or have you consider a next step to rein in some of your worries. You have to do the work. You and God are the key conduits to growth and transformation. If someone else needs to be in the equation, such as a health professional, ask God to guide you to that person.

Assume the best intentions and most sincere sentiments. This text is for everyday worriers not those with severe anxiety, panic attacks, and rehabilitating responses. In no way is the intent to trivialize the life-altering impact and struggles some suffer from to function on a daily basis. Sometimes your condition is a spiritual one and not physical. Perhaps it is a combination of the things mentioned in this book combined with a medical practitioner.

The 30-Day Writing Journey to shift from worry to peace is not . . .

A substitute for help from a practitioner. There are some burdens that are extremely heavy. There are severe situations of trauma, abuse, terminal illnesses, etc. There are also dire circumstances that require medical treatment and resources beyond the realm of this text. This book is for every-day habitual worriers who want to consider shifting your thoughts a bit.

So now let's jump in!

Bottom Line

Prayer is your primary weapon against worry. Counter worry with faith. Pray to God to increase your faith. Worry is an opportunity for your faith to grow. You have to really trust and believe in God and that he will help you through no matter the battle you face, and no matter how long it takes. Perhaps God meets us at our level of expectation. God is moving during the wait and during what appears to be silence. If you are in the pit of worry, that means there is a need for more of God in the circumstance. You build your trust through how you handle experiences. You must acknowledge your dependence on God. Fight against the satanic influence of remaining frozen in the cycle of worry and unbelief.

God had plans for your life, even before you were conceived. He has plans for you to prosper. He has set you apart from every other human on Earth. You are valuable to him. God's love is unconditional and unwavering. Cling to God and his promises to never leave you or forsake you no matter what happens. Don't you think God knows exactly what he's doing? Let go, and let God handle things. Address issues when they present themselves, and when they do, thank God in advance for clearing your path and seeing you through.

Don't forebode disaster. Reframe how you look at hardships and seasons of waiting. Keep your eyes fixed on God. Pray, study his word, and believe. Be patient and strong, loaded with prayer, and the will to get through your heightened season of worry. When feelings of worry come, don't allow them to take root in your mind. Distance your mind from the worry. Remember, God is bigger than any worry, any problem, or any lack. He loves us. He takes care of us. Ruminating over people and things is counterproductive. It doesn't result in anything. Take it battle by battle. All battles have an end date. **Many of the most challenging moments precede some of the very best moments.** Get control of your mind and your thoughts. **Completely surrender whatever it is you are worried about.** We were never intended to carry our burdens ourselves. We are not equipped to handle life without him. This is the pride–worry connection. No man can fight life's battles without God's supernatural help and provision. Submit. Give God total control. Be responsive when he reveals things to you. **You are strong and resilient.** We can endure a lot more than we could ever imagine. If we channel the feelings in the right direction, it could be a good chance to take a step back, reflect, and make important changes in our lives. Stay anchored to the vision God has for your life.

The Research and Process

In exploring these ideas, I reflected on my own life experiences and all the seasons of immense worry. My writings are birthed out of my own pain and process. I wanted to create the text I could personally refer to when worry came knocking on my door again. Life can present us with many curveballs that are so incredibly overwhelming that they instill long-lasting pain and fear. I want to be better equipped to handle each worry season and not let it keep me in a frozen or arrested state. What was the best coping mechanism to work myself out of this agitated state? I had to remain focused and bolster up my trust in God. I explore these insights and revelations in this 30-Day writing journey to shift from worry to peace.

The Structure

When I thought of a structure or format that brought me to a place of understanding in the past, I recalled a 30-Day writing challenge I had participated in a few years prior. During that time, I felt broken and confused by the cards life had dealt me. In retrospect, those cards were a true blessing. Daily writing often serves as an enlightenment ritual for me personally and lifts me out of darkness. This led me to reflect on how I could use my season of worry to increase my faith in God. This book is focused on you doing the transformative work to ease your worries. Notice there are scriptures preceding every daily entry. Meditate on these words.

The Outcome

Going through each day, one by one, strengthened my resolve to lighten the burden of worry and put my trust in God. The worries of life are still a struggle, but I know who is in control. When you are overcome with worry, remember the disciples in the Sea of Galilee. In one instant, God calmed the sea. Each storm is a reminder that God can calm anything instantly. More importantly, what is God teaching us or building us up for when he allows our storms to continue for just a little while longer? I love seeing the glory of God manifest from challenges.

Get Ready

In the subsequent pages, you will be presented with daily worry passages. This is a series of 30 reflections on worry with meditations to carry out every day. You will also be asked to write each day. Pour your heart out onto the pages that have been provided.

Read, reflect, write, and lighten your worry load. I hope that you will benefit from this 30-Day journey, and that by the end you will feel more at peace. Our passage reading and reflection plan for the next 30 days will remind us of who God is and the peace only he can provide despite our worries.

Before we get started . . .

Self-reflect

1.   Sometimes your worry increases because you haven't been spending time with God. God will get your attention one way or another. Do you believe you have been spending ample time with God? How do you plan on increasing your time with Him?

_____

_____

_____

2.   Sometimes your worry increases because you are actively and knowingly in the pit of a present sin. No one is without sin, but God will get your attention one way or another. Are you aware that you are in the midst of doing something God has revealed to you that needs to stop? Repent regarding past sin and plan on ridding yourself from active sin.

_____

_____

_____

My Worry Action Plan

Before you get into the 30-Day writing journey, I ask that you come up with a preliminary Worry Action Plan as you move throughout these next 30 days. It is a plan that will serve as your go-to response when burdened with worry. You will build on this plan as you read.

_____

_____

_____

_____

_____

_____

_____

_____

_____

_____

_____

_____

_____

_____

_____

_____

_____

_____

_____

_____

_____

_____

_____

_____

_____

_____

_____

_____

_____

_____

"Peace I leave with you; my peace I give you. I do not give to you as the world gives. **Do not let your hearts be troubled and do not be afraid.**"

— John 14:27 (NIV)

"**I can do all things** through him who gives me strength."

— Philippians 4:13 (NIV)

DAY 1

Pray and Ask God for Help

It's always wonderful to begin your day with quiet time centered on God. No matter the moment, once the worrisome feelings begin to pick up, pause and pray. **Prayer is your key weapon against worry.** Try your best to pray instead of worry. God will send his angels to guide and protect you.

When you are feeling lost or overwhelmed, turning to prayer will help ease your pain. But sometimes we are too distracted or upset, and our minds are too scattered to focus. When this happens, I like to write poetry, or what I call a "Worry Prayer." It's important to remember that God is always with us.

Lord, I come to you because I am worried.
I am concerned about the direction to take in certain areas of my life
Each pathway has a repercussion.

I know I must endure in certain challenging areas of my life
Because you have called me to be there
Only you can help me through
You have the power to change my circumstances.

I thank you for life:
All the blessings
All the circumstances

That have helped shape me to become
Better, bolder, and stronger.

It is so evident to me that you have mapped out my life
In every single detail, God.

I pray I learn to trust you more and more
To the point I can truly push some of the negative emotions to the side
Because I know I am safe in your arms.
Any perceived threats are not real
Please help my worries subside.
You are in control
Suppress my feelings of panic and fret, God.
You know the number of hairs on my head.
You had a plan for my life before my conception.
You are always with me,
And with those I love.
Have your angels protect me, my family, and friends
In our comings and goings.

Lord, if I am truly honest, right now I am concerned.
There are disasters and disease happening around me;
Family members are sick
Tension and anger abound
Life is not in my control
And that brings about worry.
I am asking for your help, Lord.
I yearn for stability
And, God, you are the great stabilizer.
You are the master protector.
With you I am safe.
I thank you for your unwavering presence
I pray for my mind to be at ease
I hope to stop mulling over the worst-case scenario

I pray for a comfort and peace.
Wrap me in your arms, Father
I feel frozen in worry
Help me to press forward
To feel safe again.

I'm not sure why certain events are transpiring
But please let your greater purpose carry out.
Lord, show me when I need to step out of the way and pray.

Lord, don't let my worries cause me to become sick;
I cannot be my best and most loving self
If I am in a heightened state of worry.
Allow me, God, to transmute my concern into action
Planning is productive
Worry shows my lack of trust in you.

Lord, allow me to not respond to everything that comes my way
I don't need to bite every dog that barks
I don't need to devote my energy to everything.

Father, forgive me for not putting my utmost trust in you.
Deliver me from this edginess
This gloom of uncertainty.
Please provide some level of relief
I cannot handle this on my own.
Please give me clarity, God
Control the negative narrative.
Join me in my circumstance, Father
Whatever happens,
I will be able to handle it
I pray to still be standing
I must remember there is an end date to this immense suffering.

Pivot my attention
To focus on you
And all the things I have neglected
By worshipping my worries
Meanwhile worry is depleting my strength.

Redirect my focus
To reduce any perceived threats
And whatever I dread the most
Lift this heavy burden, God.
Help me to relax and find safety
In your promises.
Provide a sense of security
A feeling of PEACE
Less of me, more of you
Less of me, more of you
Less of me, more of you.

Allow me to be adequately prepared for what's next
Let me be attune to the whispers you give me
Continue to guide me like a compass, God
Bring forth a miracle and change the situation
Lord, I turn it over to you.

Release me from my past
And its nagging reminders
Of what I could have done
Or what I should have done
Or what I wished would have happened.
Allow me to be hopeful and optimistic
That the future can and will be different.

Let worry not keep me frozen, God.
Rewrite the script
Give me clarity of mind

Disrupt the negative mental patterns
I've grown accustomed to imagining.
Let it be the best-case scenario
An outcome my mind cannot even fathom
Do a new thing, God
Turn my worry into trust
And my worry into faith
That all things come together for my good.

Guard my mind from spinning
While getting nowhere.
Please, God, send the right people
Remove the wrong people
Orchestrate the conditions
For us to do your will
For us to carry out your important work
With freedom
Not worry
Help me not to retaliate out of my worry and frustration.

Calm my spirit, God
Smiling in your wonder and omnipotence
Maybe life is only challenging
When I forget to submit to you
To completely surrender to you
And depend on you wholeheartedly.
Teach me the right way to live, Lord
How to achieve the peace
That only abides in you
Thank you, God, for what I know you will do
I am grateful for my life
I know I will be okay.

May I have your attention, Worry?
You will not sabotage my life

More than my own comfort.
God, please let your will be done
Thank you
Amen.

Enter every situation with prayer. Increase the frequency and intensity of your prayers over time. Shift your worries into continuous prayer, worship, and positivity. Get direction from God that this is something you should be pursuing. Then even despite the immense challenges, you can rest assured this was a God-directed assignment. Your spiritual sustenance must come from who or what God directs you to. Make sure your dependence is on God. He is with us. If we *really* trust God and really understand him and his track record, we would reduce some of our worrying.

This is a poem I like to read when I am worried . . .

Too Numb to Pray

There are times in life when you are too numb to pray
Like when my aunt died
It was like the air was taken from my breath
I was too numb to pray

I've been praying and pleading
And the enemy has hit me with just about everything
And the plastic smile will no longer suffice
I've become too numb to pray

And then I look up and see the sun shining
The various plants and flowers and insects
So perfect
So serene
So tranquil
Gratitude is prayer

Being grateful for where you are
And that you are still standing
This too shall pass
But in the eye of the storm, it feels like the storm lasts forever

And then I think about so many disasters
And how so many have lost everything
I must remind myself . . .
It's going to be okay
God has it all figured out
One day at a time
Never be too numb to pray

Day 1 Prompt: Write your own Worry Prayer on the lines below. Obeying God's instructions that he reveals to you through prayer is key to reducing your worry. What is he telling you to do? Pray and leave the rest to him.

_____

_____

_____

_____

_____

_____

_____

_____

_____

_____

_____

_____

_____

_____

_____

_____

_____

_____

_____

_____

_____

_____

_____

_____

_____

_____

_____

_____

_____

_____

_____

_____

_____

"**Cast your cares on the Lord and he will sustain you**; he will never let the righteous be shaken."

— Psalm 55:22 (NIV)

"For the Spirit **God gave us does not make us timid**, but gives us power, love and self-discipline."

— 2 Timothy 1:7 (NIV)

"Be strong and courageous. **Do not be afraid or terrified because of them**, for the Lord your God goes with you; he will never leave you nor forsake you."

— Deuteronomy 31:6 (NIV)

DAY 2

Consider the Best-Case Scenario

Our imagination is wild. This can be good and it can be bad. Worry robs us of happiness and connecting to others positively. Worry distorts hope and feelings of the future. Worry makes it easy to nose-dive into the worst-case scenario. There are times it is challenging to live with hope and optimism when you don't see the "how." You may ask, "How will God make my situation work out for my good?"

Really check in with yourself. You may ask, "Why am I feeling so uneasy? How is this uneasy feeling manifesting in my life?" Write down everything that is making you worried. Get your worries out of your mind and on to paper. What is the best-case scenario? What would be the most ideal outcome? What condition would make you feel most at ease? You must obey when God responds to you. This might mean giving up key relationships and other major moves that will be difficult and painful. What is on the other side of this sacrifice will blow your mind.

Once you truly engage in this exercise, what you write is essentially a prayer to God for what you hope will happen. Tell God your worries out loud. It's an opportunity to solicit his help in the matter. Try to look at your worries from the perspective of a third-person observer. What are your worries revealing to you? When I engage in this exercise, I get ideas of things I can do to ease my worries. For example, if I am worried about my health, once I write that down, I might get motivated to prepare my meals for the following day. Trust that God will guide you to what's best, and only he can do even better than your best-case scenario.

Day 2 Prompt: In the first column, write down all of your worries. There are 6 rows to write your worries, but don't feel like you have to fill them all out.

In the second column, write down the best-case scenario, and set your intentions for the best-case scenario. Then, if things don't work out the way you want them to, you have to trust that you will be okay.

In the third column, begin with the phrase, "I will be okay . . ." You might even consider adding, "And maybe it will all be a blessing," or, "And I believe God for a miracle." Count this as your designated worry time: a time you are giving these worries to God in surrender.

After you have filled out your Worry Chart, say the following prayer: "God, here are my worries. I pray that you calm my mind. I trust you and know that whatever the outcome, it will work out for my good. I release all negative foreboding and expectations. Amen."

	Worries (prayers)	Best-Case Scenario: Set your intention	What happens if things don't work out the way you want them to? Begin with the phrase, "I will be okay . . ." You can also add in, "And maybe it will all be a blessing," or, "And I believe God for a miracle."
Example	Money	We get on a budget: cook more, save, invest.	I will be okay. I will do my best. I will educate myself on how to create a budget. I will exercise discipline when shopping for personal reasons. Maybe my journey with money will prove to be a blessing.

1			
2			
3			
4			
5			
6			

"I sought the Lord, and he answered me;
he delivered me from all my fears."

— Psalm 34:4 (NIV)

"Fear thou not; for **I am with thee**:
be not dismayed; for I am thy God:
I will strengthen thee; yea, I will help thee;
yea, I will uphold thee with the right hand of my righteousness."

— Isaiah 41:10 (NIV)

DAY 3

Accept your Human Limitations

Humble Submission

Life is challenging. Life becomes extra challenging when we do not rely on God. The weight of the world and our own individual burdens were never intended to be carried alone. God wants us to reach out to him. God wants us to know we can depend on him. He wants a personal relationship with us, and he wants us to know we can rely and depend on him. Spend time with God and genuinely get to know him and deepen your relationship with him.

Day 1 was a day of prayer and a declaration. Day 3 is also a day of prayer, but it is to pray with humility and submission. Bow down. Accept your human limitations. Don't just go through the motions of prayer—really submit to God's will deep in your mind, body, and spirit. Freely allow God to work. Stop doing life's challenges all by yourself. Pray in a way that acknowledges your dependence on God and your faith in God. He will send the right people to assist you. Don't become overly self-sufficient.

Much of the worry we experience can subside with prayer. "God please rid me of this feeling. Show me the way. Calm my spirit. What should I do, Lord?" God doesn't necessarily remove us from the challenging circumstance, but he will certainly join us and protect us in the circumstance. God will point you in the right direction. He will show you exactly what needs to be taken care of, what conversations you need to have, what habits you have to rein in, and what calming practices you need to incorporate in your life. He will direct your path to feeling less tension.

There have been many times that I have just prayed my way through situations that caused a heightened feeling of worry. Feelings of worry come up when I am in situations that are new or unexpected, where I have little background knowledge, and when I have to navigate new terrain. In these moments, God will direct me to someone who has experience in the area, or simply get me through despite my limitations. After praying and making the key moves and having the key conversations God directs me to have, God tends to direct me to a point of peaceful surrender. I'm left with a feeling that no matter what happens, God has me in the palm of his hands. With God on my side, I will be okay.

Fasting

As I explained in my book, *Armored Up: A 30-Day Writing Journey to Combat Spiritual Warfare,* I discuss fasting. "Fasting involves voluntarily abstaining from certain pleasures, oftentimes food. It is a submission of our flesh. During this time, increase your prayer and focus on the spirit. Consider praying hourly. It is a time to draw nearer to God and to increase our faith and the power of your prayers.

Fasting is for a purpose. It intensifies prayer and sets you up to receive more from God. It reveals our idols and who we are turning to or dependent on other than God. Remember, work, spouse, or a child is not our God. God is our God.

We often forget the sacrifice that is involved when asking God for a breakthrough. This demonstrates our yearning for God. Approach God with humility and a repenting heart. Demonstrate an openness and willingness to hear from God and a true devotion to him.

Fasting is an experience that can produce miracles. It humbles us and reminds us of our dependence on God and prepares us for His response. Expect healing in your area of prayer, a renewed focus on God, and answered prayers. There are certain things that can only come to pass or be revealed through fasting and prayer. Fasting should also extend out to doing good for others.

There are various types of fasts, so do your research and do what works for you. Maybe it's food, or maybe it's from various distractions in your life. No matter which fast you adhere to, plan on giving more of your time to God.

When God reveals your next steps to you, be sure to follow in obedience. What feedback is our circumstance giving us? What is the universe trying to tell us?"

Day 3 Prompt: Have you been carrying the weight of your burdens alone? In what ways do you see pride and lack of humility as a contributor to your tension? What can you do today as an act of submission? Have you tried to drastically increase your prayer life?

_____
_____
_____
_____
_____
_____
_____
_____
_____
_____
_____
_____
_____
_____
_____
_____
_____
_____
_____
_____
_____
_____
_____
_____
_____
_____
_____
_____
_____
_____
_____
_____
_____

"Cast all your anxiety on him because **he cares for you**."

— 1 Peter 5:7 (NIV)

One day Jesus said to his disciples, "Let us go over to the other side of the lake." So they got into a boat and set out. As they sailed, he fell asleep. A squall came down on the lake, so that the boat was being swamped, and they were in great danger.

The disciples went and woke him, saying, "Master, Master, we're going to drown!"

He got up and rebuked the wind and the raging waters; the storm subsided, and all was calm. **"Where is your faith?"** he asked his disciples.

In fear and amazement they asked one another, "Who is this? He commands even the winds and the water, and they obey him."

— Luke 8:22–25 (NIV)

DAY 4

Have Faith and Trust in God

Like the disciples in the boat, we cannot avoid the storms of life, but know that God is with us. An example of worrying would sound like, "God, I don't really believe you can handle this." Believe God has it ALL covered and under his control. Trust him. Show that you are dependent on God. Have faith and hope in the future. What God has for you is for you. Continue to pray and believe your worries will subside and God will work it out. Trust God and not the odds that are against you or the appearance of the situation.

We are worried because we are aware we are not in control, but we should be rest assured that God is. We all want certainty, but that is not the essence of faith. The essence of faith is believing in the midst of uncertainty. These are the key moments our faith is strengthened. No matter what happens, say, "This will not take me under."

God had a plan for your life, even before you were conceived. Your entire life has been mapped out.

He counts the hairs on your head.

You are his prized jewel.

You are the apple of his eye.

He has your name engraved in the palm of his hand.

He is the same God who said, "Let there be light," and then there was light.

For these reasons and more, we should prioritize increasing our faith and trust in him.

As stated in my book, *Armored Up: A 30 Day Writing Journey to Combat Spiritual Warfare,* "Despite what external circumstances tell us, we have to believe God can do what he says he will do. We don't know how God will get us out. That is where faith steps in. If there is anything you must do immediately, you must build and expand your faith. You have to be still and remember who God is. He is still on the throne. He will work all things out for your good. TRUST that he will get you through it. TRUST that he will use whatever you endure to glorify his name. All things work together for good. ALL THINGS. There is opportunity wrapped in every storm. There is purpose in your pain. God can turn our persecution into a victory.

We are often toggling between fear, stress, and faith at any given time, but there is no need to fear. Tell yourself, "[Your name] I am safe. I have nothing to fear. I am safe." When God moves, we will know it was God. Pray. Trust God. Act as if it is so. Have aggressive expectations. Don't dress rehearse bad news. Get extremely hopeful. Have faith he will see you through. Has he ever abandoned you before? God will protect you. There is no need to retaliate. He is an on-time God. Rejoice even in the midst of adversities. Keep your eyes focused on God at all times. Take things one step at a time, one whisper from God at a time. When family members are sick, we have to have faith they will get better. When we are out of work, we have to have faith the right job will come along. When we are at our wit's end with certain family relationships, we must have faith that our relationships will be restored. God may appear to play along as a chess player in the game of life, but he controls the entire chess board. He will turn all of Satan's moves for our benefit. God made the ultimate chess move when he sent his son to die for our sins, and although Jesus died on the cross, he rose again! Checkmate! He's got us completely covered by his blood. With faith, we can overcome anything! If God is for us, who can be against us?"

The following is a poem about doubt.

When did I allow doubt to take root?
I know his past faithfulness
I know what his word says
I choose to believe in God
And his promises
So how did I let doubt creep in?

Allow your faith to birth new hope, remembering that God allows all things to work together for our good—*all things.* His nuanced plan is far greater and more intricate than our minds can fathom. If not hope in our future here on Earth, look forward to eternity when all believers will be joined as one, and all pain and suffering will be gone.

Day 4 Prompt: Check in with your belief versus your faith. If you are reading this book, I can surmise you have some belief in God. Do you trust God? What are past examples where God has demonstrated he loves and adores you? What would be different this time?

_____

_____

_____

_____

_____

_____

_____

_____

_____

_____

_____

_____

_____

_____

_____

_____

_____

_____

_____

_____

_____

_____

_____

_____

_____

_____

_____

_____

_____

_____

_____

_____

_____

"For **as he thinketh in his heart**, so is he . . ."

— Proverbs 23:7 (King James Version)

DAY 5

Distract Yourself with Positivity

Shift your mind and thoughts. Pivot your attention. Come up with a list of things that can help to take your mind off the things that have you worried. Think of positive ways of distracting yourself from the worry. There is more to life than whatever is making you worrisome. Have hopeful anticipation for each day. Treat life as one big adventure. Always believe that something wonderful will happen every day. The following are strategies to shift your thoughts and energy in a more positive direction.

1. Find positive therapeutic outlets.
2. Search for beauty—around your home, outside, in music, in literature, etc.
3. Feed your mind by getting mentally busy or reading books.
4. Watch motivational videos and podcasts.
5. Delve into personal projects. Plan and execute.
6. Instead of worrying and expecting the worst, get curious. Become curious about solving a particular problem.
7. Consider something you need to work on in the area of self-improvement.
8. Get creative.
9. Listen to someone else's testimony.
10. Listen to a sermon.
11. Cook!

12. Sign up for a class. Learn something new. I find I am less worried when I feel I'm growing and evolving.
13. Distract yourself with other topics.
14. Create art in the form of painting and poetry. Buy an adult coloring book.
15. Be like a child again: bounce on a trampoline or play hide-and-seek.
16. Learn a new language.
17. Explore a space you have never explored.
18. Reconnect with a long-lost friend.
19. Walk around your home and list the tasks that need to get done, then dive in.
20. Tap into the power of music—sing, dance, or do both!
21. Take a moment to focus on the good and positive things around you.
22. What makes you happy? Whatever it is, do more of it.
23. Contribute to the happiness of those around you.
24. Connect with others.

Shift your focus to God and something interesting. Learn, grow, build, create, and be expansive in every sense of the word. When you are in an expansive state, worry seems to not be as much of a priority. When you are wallowing, you remain in the pit of worry. There is often heightened creativity during worrisome seasons. It is difficult to worry and create simultaneously. Learning and creating is a positive distraction away from our worries.

Day 5 Prompt: What are sources of inspiration you can tap into to shift your worries?

Your homework is the following:

1. Reread your Day 1 Worry Prayer.
2. Give thanks.
3. Update your Worry Action Plan.
4. Intentionally think and act positively. Pick at least one item from the Day 5 list each day and engage in it wholeheartedly. Be sure to remain present as you engage in the activity and feel all the joy.

Sheryl Walker

"Give thanks to the Lord, for he is good;
his love endures forever."

— Psalm 118:1 (NIV)

DAY 6

Practice Gratitude

Gratitude

Despite the many situations that can make us worried, we have a lot to be grateful for. There are so many people in really dire situations. If we wake up every day able to move our bodies, with our basic needs met, and people who love us, we are truly blessed. We must count our blessings. Look around at your life and all God has done.

I find that even in the most challenging situations, there is ALWAYS an ounce of beauty, a speckle of hope. God always makes himself known. It could be a breakthrough to a situation, or an unexpected angel that walks into our lives. God really does love us and has our best interest in heart, even through our worries.

If I am worried about a person or situation, I like to focus on what I appreciate about that person or circumstance, and my perspective changes.

Say the following out loud. Truly rejoice!
Thank you, God, for all my blessings.
Thank you, God, for the small things.
Thank you, God, for allowing me to reframe the unfavorable.
Thank you, God, for miracles.
Thank you, God, for your perfect timing.

Thank you, God, for the angels you place in our lives.

Thank you, God, that life is working for me and not against me.

Thank you, God, for places and spaces that feel like home.

Thank you, God, for breath and good health.

Thank you, God, for opportunities to affirm, bless, and serve others with good.

Thank you, God, for places and spaces that can handle my enormity

Thank you, God, for patience so that I can cease complaining and wait well.

Thank you, God, for expressions of love and care.

Thank you, God, for reasons to smile and be happy.

Thank you, God, for sacred moments of joy with loved ones.

Thank you, God, for your companionship out of the darkness and into the light.

Thank you, God, for the gift of prayer.

Thank you, God, for planting the dream and bringing it to fruition.

Thank you, God, for authentic connections.

Thank you, God, for giving me peace.

Thank you, God, for making your presence known.

Thank you, God, for EVERYTHING.

Perspective

In my book, *More Grateful: A 21-Day Writing Journey to Increase Gratitude,* I discuss perspective-shifting statements. These statements shift what is perceived as a negative situation into gratitude. Put a chokehold on worry as soon as it enters your mind.

Here are a few examples of perspective-shifting statements:

Negative statement: "My child is frustrating me."

Perspective-shifting statement: "Well, I have a child. I acknowledge that many people wish they could have a child."

Negative statement: "This person is upsetting me."

Perspective-shifting statement: "When I consider the kindness they showed me during my own struggles, I feel gratitude in my heart and release the animosity I feel right now. What they have given me is more than enough."

Other Strategies

Thank God and press forward: When something bad does not occur and you've dodged a bullet, so to speak, it's important to thank God and press forward. For example, as a parent, things happen all the time. When our children are okay and the circumstances could have fared much worse, we must say, "Thank you God, thank you angels," and press forward. At the appropriate time, spend time devising preventative measures and non-threating ways to address the situation.

List all the "good" that came out of the "bad": When I think about the most challenging moments in life, there have been amazing opportunities birthed out of the pain. For example, new insights and awareness have led to me sharing that knowledge with others. The bitter sting of loss has allowed me to be a resource and support for others enduring the same painful situation. Challenging situations have allowed me to spend more time with my family, which has been priceless. As I've talked to others, they have shared their own opportunities that were birthed out of loss, like losing a job and that being a blessing in disguise because they were able to spend time with their sibling before they passed, or how they were able to travel the world for an extended period of time. I don't know about you, but this leaves me in a state of awe. God, you ALWAYS turn things around in my favor. Why do I get so upset? Why do I question you? God allows things that are beyond logic and reasoning, but pain is always for purpose. Something is always birthed from pain.

This reminds me of my favorite haiku by Mizuta Masahide: "Barn's burnt down . . . now I can see the moon."

Day 6 Prompt 1: What are some fortunate aspects of your life? What are you feeling especially grateful for right now? Consider someone who is in a dire situation and pray for them. Count your blessings. Also consider one of your greatest worries. What do you appreciate about that person or situation? What is a perspective-shifting statement you could regularly state?

_____

_____

_____

_____

_____

_____

_____

_____

_____

_____

_____

_____

_____

_____

_____

_____

_____

_____

_____

_____

_____

_____

_____

_____

_____

_____

_____

Day 6 Prompt 2: In *More Grateful,* I introduce the Gratitude T-Chart. Here is how it works: For one week, take notice of all your blessings—big and small—and all your frustrations. On the left side, track all the good things you take notice of. On the right side, track how the enemy attempted to discourage you but it worked out. You will see that God is really for you and making moves on your behalf during this worry season. There is a lot more that is in your favor than you might be seeing. What God is doing is far greater than the devil's tactics.

Gratitude T-Chart

BLESSINGS	ATTEMPTS AT DISCOURAGEMENT

Your homework:

1. Reread your Day 1 Worry Prayer
2. Give thanks
3. Update your Worry Action Plan
4. Intentionally think and act positively

"When I am afraid, **I put my trust in you**."

— Psalm 56:3 (NIV)

"So we say with confidence, **The Lord is my helper**; I will not be afraid. What can mere mortals do to me?"

— Hebrews 13:6 (NIV)

DAY 7

Self-Care to Achieve Peace

On the plane, they say in cases of emergency to put the oxygen mask on yourself first before putting the mask on anyone else. You must take care of you to be able to care for anyone else. Caring for yourself during worrisome seasons is critical. You come first. In the following sections, I have provided examples of ways that you can practice self-care.

1. Take breaks and rest

Even if it is five minutes, take mini-breaks to reset, regroup, and re-center. A simple walk outside might just be the reprieve you need. A longer more restorative season of doing less might also be necessary.

Don't underestimate the power of more restorative sleep. Try going to bed a little earlier or incorporate naps.

Plan uninterrupted "me" days where you focus on your personal restoration and replenishment.

2. Move toward peace

We need moments of peace, solitude, and quiet time. This could be as simple as sitting in a coffee shop. On day 14, I discuss getting organized to get things in motion, but there is also something to be said of slowing down one's pace and remaining still.

Create a sanctuary in your home or engage in peace-inducing practices such as deep breathing exercises, a warm bath, meditation, yoga, massage with essential oils, reflexology, or acupuncture. Treating yourself to a manicure or having your makeup done and getting dressed can work wonders. Incorporate your own calming rituals. Read books and passages that bring you a sense of calm.

Some of the most peaceful moments also include watching snow or rain fall. Long, quiet walks can be magical.

Moving toward peace could literally mean moving to another city, state, or even country. You could go on a vacation, or at minimum a stay-cation.

Then there are those who seem to be angels and bring you peace and support when you are in their presence. Increase your time with those individuals.

Babies and puppies are also great to be around.

And then there is the peace that only lives within God.

3. Move toward love

Sometimes when we are riddled with unfavorable thoughts and circumstances, perhaps the direction we ought to be moving is toward more love. What can you do that is an expression of love toward someone else? How can you be more loving to yourself?

What is your love language? For example, if it is physical touch and you have not been held or received a hug in a while, see where your need for love can be met that is both appropriate and spiritually guided.

4. Move toward health

Prioritize wellness. Eat clean and well, and move your body with intention. Take notice if certain highly allergenic foods increase your worry. Again, get enough restorative sleep (dark space), hydrate, and move toward better work-life balance. Practice mindfulness, such as mindful eating, which is a way to focus on the present and the foods you are actually consuming. Monitor your consumption of excess sugar, starches, gluten, wheat, and alcohol. Eat more foods that are deemed to have anti-worry properties such as blueberries and bananas. Talk to a health (holistic) practitioner about magnesium, vitamin D, vitamin B-complex, Vitamin K, removing amalgam fillings, and improving your gut health. Delve deeper into your hormones and other potential imbalances. Remove toxins in the form of fragrances and home products.

5. Move toward power

Whatever it is that will make you step into your power, do that. Maybe it is speaking up and taking a stand. Maybe it is becoming more vulnerable. Maybe it is leaving an abusive relationship once and for all. Maybe it is getting serious about your health and fitness routine or the budget you have been meaning to create and adhere to. As it pertains to worry, maybe your power is putting a full stop to worrisome thoughts and literally kicking worry to the curb. "Listen, Worry, you will not waste any more of my time and sabotage my life." For me, having a technique when my worry rises, makes me feel powerful. I've been relying heavily on deep breathing techniques and short focused prayer at the height of my worry.

6. Restrict access to the people and things that bring forth stress and wrestle with your spirit

There are some individuals or external stimuli that increase your worry and agitation. There is a pattern to their behavior. There might be constant digs and condescending remarks. They feel like emotional terrorists. Intentionally or unintentionally, they play certain games to toy with your emotions. They will weaken and deplete you over time. Even worse, you might begin behaving as they do.

They might be struggling right now with their own personal issues and may have many unresolved struggles from the past. How can you love them while creating a boundary and restricting access to ensure that you are emotionally safe?

Reprogram how you respond to or view agitators or your past situation. People who constantly provoke others with negativity have suffered and are continuing to suffer. Try not to judge them and have compassion, but prioritize self-care. Move away from people who make you feel emotionally unsafe. Silence is an appropriate response. Be still. Ask God, "Is this a close relationship, a "love from a distance" situation, or someone who should not be in my life at all?" Ignore the peanut gallery— those who are quick to assess and judge but aren't putting themselves out there to make bold moves in their life.

You are the gatekeeper to who or what you let into your mind. Limit your contact. Limit their access to you. Change how you interpret, process, and personalize their words and actions. Have boundaries. If they are not adjusting, limiting access might be the change you need to implement. There might come a day you can engage with them, but for right now, time, space, and limited access is needed.

Don't respond to everything that comes your way. There is a famous saying, "Don't bite every dog that barks." Some people intentionally increase your worry as a way to try to control and manipulate you.

I also find listening to the news or being on social media too much contributes to worry. There is a lot happening in the world that is upsetting and traumatic, so it's important to limit your access to these platforms. You must be the gatekeeper and protect the stories that are allowed to enter your mind.

7. Change your daily habits with positive coping mechanisms

Worry in and of itself is a bad habit, and your habits control your life, good and bad. If excess worry is your stress response, you have to work to uproot that. Maybe your coping responses started in childhood or are a result of later hurts and pains. Work on healing.

If your habits promote worry instead of peace, you will be more worried. For example, if much of your day is spent with people you are constantly in conflict with, naturally your stress and anxieties will be heightened. If your daily habit is to numb out with unhealthy coping mechanisms, such as drugs or alcohol, that is not moving in the direction of a positive and healthy lifestyle.

Learn techniques to bring yourself down off the worry ledge. This could be a combination of deep breathing techniques and repeating the mantra, "I am safe. God is with me." There could be many practices that move you to a more peaceful place such as taking a walk or jog in nature, or improving your diet and exercise. Consider journaling, listening to uplifting messages, talking to someone, or reading a self-help book. Practice rejecting negative thoughts as soon as they come in. Remember, no matter the worry, "this too shall pass."

8. Handle yourself with care

We have the potential to do great damage during high-stress seasons of life. Give yourself extra grace and move more delicately through high-stress seasons. Don't make key decisions when depleted.

Shift from being a multi-tasker to a single tasker. Do less.

Refuse to be stirred up by new drama. If you are reacting in anger or snapping at others, it might be an indication that you need to put yourself in time-out. Take a break and re-engage when you are back to baseline.

9. Lean into negative emotions you have to move through

We often try to avoid sadness or grief. Often, we must allow ourselves the space to feel that depth of sorrow, process, and heal. Avoiding the hard work will certainly add to your worry. For example, if someone betrayed you or didn't support you as you would have liked, you can feel disappointed, but then you can work to let go of those negative emotions and move on.

10. Be mindful of what gets your energy

Do you give yourself sacred time? It's important to strategically block the absorption of negative information. Don't absorb everything that comes your way when it presents itself. For example, if your boss decides he or she wants to give your annual feedback at a time when you are already depleted and extra worried, postpone reading it in detail until you are at baseline and ready to receive it.

Exercise the discipline to not absorb everything that comes your way. Be disciplined and carve out sacred, restricted time throughout your day. Sometimes our attempts to pray and alleviate our worries are interrupted by our busy schedules and open accessibility through smartphones and text messages. For example, when I'm reading my Bible, I try not to check texts. I want to be focused. One wrong message could distract and completely derail me. We can instantly take on even more worries. What do you allow to be dropped at your mental doorstep without your approval? Commit to honoring your sacred time.

Also, you will have to deliberately ignore some things people say and do. You will have to give a lot of grace for a lot of mistakes and missteps because you will be depleted if everything gets your attention. Everything does not deserve your energy. There are moments you have to thank God and the angels of protection when you dodge a bullet, so to speak, and a misstep or mistake does not result in something even worse.

Day 7 Prompt: In what ways are you moving toward peace? What do you plan on doing soon to increase your peace? What boundary do you need to put in place? What daily habit is increasing your worry?

_____

_____

_____

_____

_____

_____

_____

_____

_____

_____

_____

_____

_____

_____

_____

_____

_____

_____

_____

_____

_____

_____

_____

_____

Your homework:

1. Reread your Day 1 Worry Prayer
2. Give thanks
3. Update your Worry Action Plan
4. Intentionally think and act positively

Sheryl Walker

"In the same way, **let your light shine before others**, that they may see your good deeds and glorify your Father in heaven."

— Matthew 5:16 (NIV)

DAY 8

Do Good Things for Others

We all know the feeling of worry. We all know when life feels out of control. We all know how peaceful it is when our mind is finally at ease. Why not gift someone else with that feeling through the expression of kindness in some form?

See your personal worry as an opportunity to be a blessing to others and reduce their worry even in the midst of your own. Cut someone some slack, lend a helping hand, serve others with your gifts, or just be a listening ear. Give your time. Show up. Encourage. All of those gestures could help to alleviate someone else's worry in some way.

Giving the gift of service has a renewing quality. Many people literally feel better when they serve. When you genuinely share your gifts and story, you bless someone else and in turn become blessed. Be sure to balance out helping occasionally versus enabling or being a doormat for a prolonged period of time.

Give the love, acceptance, and validation to all. Cast your love net vast and wide. For example, you may want to consider: "How can I love [insert name] more today? How can I show this love explicitly?"

The Law of Reaping and Sowing

It is important to focus on the seeds you are planting in a situation. It is the focus on the seeds that will impact the harvest. It's all about the seeds. Be less concerned about the harvest. What seeds are you sowing?

Sheryl Walker

How are you tilling the land? What are you doing in the now? If you bring your best self to the cultivation of the seeds, the harvest will be profound. The harvest will eventually come. It may not be now or in your lifetime, but the harvest will come if you sow the right seeds. Sometimes we don't see the fruits of our labor until way past our time. Sow the seeds. Focus on the seeds.

Day 8 Prompt: What are opportunities to do good and reduce someone else's worry even in the midst of your own? What are ways you can try not to trigger worry in others? What good seeds are you sowing?

_____

_____

_____

_____

_____

_____

_____

_____

_____

_____

_____

_____

_____

_____

_____

_____

_____

_____

_____

_____

_____

_____

_____

Your homework:

1.　Reread your Day 1 Worry Prayer
2.　Give thanks
3.　Update your Worry Action Plan
4.　Intentionally think and act positively

DAY 9

Get Help

Getting your worries off your chest helps. Worry isolates us, so it is good to have conversations with others. Sometimes saying things out loud helps to process the things that are on your mind. The right friend, coach, and/or therapist could be great ongoing support. Ask God to direct you to the key people and conversations that could help to alleviate some of your worry and provide you with wisdom.

1. Talk to an expert on the subject area

Whatever you are worried about, there is someone you can turn to who is an expert in that field or can offer insight. There is great power when you have smart conversations with well-informed people. For example, if you are worried about finding a new job, a friend who just landed a new job after months of searching might be a great person to talk to. Talk to someone who is in the thick of the same situation. Talk to someone who has expertise in the area where you are less experienced. Gaining their perspective and insight might alleviate some of your worry.

2. Ask for help

There are so many skilled people out there. If you need help with certain tasks around your home or help with your children so you can take a mental break, solicit help. The right, trusted help can be such a great relief. If you are struggling with eating well and exercising, see if there is an affordable nutritionist or exercise professional who can coach you. We were meant to lean on the gifts and talents of others.

The Bible tells us to ask and we shall receive. We have not, because we ask not. I've found it pretty amazing how the help often comes, and many times in unexpected forms, if only I just ask for help.

3. Process your pain

Talking through your worry might mean making sense of your past with the help of a professional. Sometimes we don't even understand we were traumatized until we begin the conversation. A lot of our worries stem from our unhealed inner child. I will repeat that: *A lot of our worries stem from our unhealed inner child.* Unprocessed aspects of your life can also serve as a hurdle or as a weapon to hurt others. Don't stop yourself from seeking help and learning positive tools and coping mechanisms.

Balance your conversations with others with what God is telling you to do. I remember when I was ready to make a career change and everyone had an opinion. I knew God was telling me the opposite of most of the opinions I had heard from family and friends. The decision from God was the best decision. Even though those giving me the advice knew me and loved me, God's voice had to supersede all the other voices.

When new pain comes upon you, try to let it not penetrate you. Imagine pain not even touching you, but pain falling to the ground and you stepping over it. After you step over it, keep your head held high and keep moving.

4. Discuss the elephant in the room

To alleviate your worries, you might need to have key conversations you have been avoiding. It may be time to end being passive. Eliminate avoidance. Speak up. Address the elephant in the room under God's guidance and timing. You can say just about anything with prayer beforehand, the right framing, and adequate grace. A book that has helped me not only in my relationships but with having difficult conversations is *Listen, Learn, Love* by Susie Miller. It is a simple concept but yields transformational results.

You might also have to own up to your part in your own heightened worry, such as resenting other people's success or deflecting what you perceive to be life's missed opportunities. Pray and follow God's direction.

If your coping mechanism has been less than ideal, such as drugs or alcohol, it might be time to fill your toolkit with more positive mechanisms.

5. Talk to an elder or reconnect with a friend

Sometimes we don't want to share our worries with friends, but just talking to a friend, catching up, and hearing about their life might inadvertently shift your energy. Just hearing their voice can bring forth nostalgic feelings. Also, there is something about hearing a new voice that can break us out of the lull and monotony of dwelling. You might also consider connecting with an elder. Their wisdom is priceless. There is much that can be gleaned from a simple conversation.

6. Connect with your community, family, or "tribe"

Life is all about relationships. Try not to be alone in your worries. Find a group of people that you feel connected to, where you feel understood and accepted for who you are, and value your presence. This is a place that feels like "home" or your "fit." This should be a space where you can feel vulnerable. Vulnerability with safety, love, and acceptance builds relationship. Many people feel they haven't found their tribe, but look around. They are there. It could be your immediate family. It could be your job or a church community. It could be a virtual community. Go where the love is. Move in the direction of where your heart expands and smiles. Don't underestimate the power of connection. On the contrary, move away from people who are toxic, negative, and destructive. Love them from a distance.

Day 9 Prompt: Consider your top three worries. Is there a key conversation you could have with someone to help you process your thoughts out loud? Flesh out the key questions you have for this person and the specific area of clarity you are seeking. Make the call. Schedule the appointment. Take notes below. What revelations did you have as a result of the call? Do you have to own up to an aspect of your heightened worry you are contributing to? How do you begin to process or heal that aspect of your life? Do you need physical help with a task or project? Just ask.

_____

_____

_____

_____

_____

_____

_____

_____

_____

_____

_____

_____

_____

_____

_____

_____

_____

_____

Your homework:

1. Reread your Day 1 Worry Prayer
2. Give thanks
3. Update your Worry Action Plan
4. Intentionally think and act positively

"When anxiety was great within me,
your consolation brought me joy."

— Psalm 94:19 (NIV)

DAY 10

Check your Pride

There is a pride–worry connection. When we think our accomplishments are due to ourselves or that we can handle everything alone; this puts us in a complicated situation. What happens when our human strength no longer proves to be reliable? We worry. We have to truly believe God gets all the credit and all the glory for the good in our lives.

If you are focused on your strength and what you can do in your limited human ability, you will have more worry. It's not for us to do by ourselves. We alone will not save the world. It's God. God uses your strengths and everyone else's to carry out his work. Reach out to God and let him help. He will show you who else can help. Maybe it's bringing a team of people to help. He will direct you to the right resource. Humble yourself and respect God's authority. Humbly ask, "I really need help, God. Will you please intercede?" When the blessing comes, give him the glory. Everything we are capable of is from God. Every good thing is from God.

Day 10 Prompt: Are you one to quickly give God the glory, or do you take credit for the things that go well? Reflect on your personal phrasing of things. Instead of saying, "**I** completed the _____ and that led to my success," say this instead, "Thank you, **God,** for directing my path and showing me _____. Thank you, God, for allowing me to be successful."

_____

Your homework:

1. Reread your Day 1 Worry Prayer
2. Give thanks
3. Update your Worry Action Plan
4. Intentionally think and act positively

"'For **I know the plans I have for you**,' declares the Lord, 'plans to prosper you and not to harm you, plans to give you hope and a future.'"

— Jeremiah 29:11 (NIV)

DAY 11

Reframe How You Look at Situations

What if God were to say to you: "[*Your name*], this experience is going to be a tough one. You will feel exhausted and at your wit's end, but hang in there. I need you to experience this so that you can [*insert goal*] and for you to be there for so and so when they go through the same thing. I need you to understand that dimension of pain, disappointment, and sorrow, and your dependence on me for a later assignment I have for you. Also, this experience is going to make you an even better person, spouse, parent, and one day grandparent. This will have a positive impact on all the generations. I had to make you so uncomfortable that you got into gear with completing [*insert God's purpose*] to fulfill the purpose I have for your life. Because of that experience, you are much more [*insert super characteristic or quality*]. There are times I have to pull you away and have my one-on-one time to really grow and develop you into all you can be. If you are not processing my message, then I make you repeat the lesson. Oh, also: I especially picked you because you are one of my stronger children. I have a few lost sheep, and you know how I feel about my lost sheep—they must return to the flock—so I entangled you in that situation as part of my strategy to help bring my lost sheep back to me. Thank you. Don't worry, I'm going to bless you with [*insert blessing*] as a way of showing you that the situation had a divine purpose."

Remember everything is wonderful if you can learn and grow from it in a profound way. Sometimes you go through pain to benefit others. God will never leave you. Your pain will prove to have purpose. This takes a great deal of spiritual maturity to accept suffering and view it from the lens of fulfilling God's will. Pray for this level of maturation as you endure your season of worry.

Day 11 Prompt: Rewrite the above hypothetical example of what God could say to you, but insert your name and information. Expand upon it.

_____

_____

_____

_____

_____

_____

_____

_____

_____

_____

_____

_____

_____

_____

_____

_____

_____

_____

_____

_____

_____

_____

_____

_____

Your homework:

1. Reread your Day 1 Worry Prayer
2. Give thanks
3. Update your Worry Action Plan
4. Intentionally think and act positively

DAY 12

Focus on the Present

Being present is everything. Get obnoxiously present. Are you dwelling on a current threat or a past and/or future worry? Stop thinking and overthinking or fall into the "analysis paralysis" trap. Only focus on what is in front of you. Be in the moment with God. Let everything else be. Don't try to hurry or worry life along. This might be the best in comparison to what is to come. During my greatest attacks of worry, I fast, pray, and get obnoxiously present. You don't know the length of this present season of uncertainty, so don't waste away time in a state of worry.

Your power is in the now. Try to live day by day, hour by hour, moment by moment. This will make up the sum total of your life. When you begin to dwell on past hurts you inflicted or were inflicted on you or anticipate the future, refocus yourself to the present. It's easy to continue ruminating over the past and overly emphasizing the what-ifs of the future. What about the right now? This very second? There are most likely no threats coming in. And even if there are, you can get through it. All is probably well in the right now.

Our mind can do some interesting things, and spiritual warfare is real. The enemy will plant a negative seed, and we can easily go plummeting down a variety of scenarios. You can waste mental energy comparing yourself to others or wishing things were a different way. Now is all you have. If you have been worrying for a while, you are pretty much a member of the Professional Worriers club and may unconsciously worry habitually as if you were on autopilot.

We must always remember that God is here, right now, and at all times. Love is always at your disposal. Look up and around. How can you be more loving to yourself or those around you?

We have to be sufficiently keen and in tune with God that we see the small moments he shows his face. Be present.

If you are worried at this very moment, breathe. Thank God. Plead for help. Identify God in this very moment. He is waiting for us to ask him for his help and to make his presence known.

Make the most of your day. Set your intention for how you want your day to be. Do small things on a daily basis to move in the direction of changing the situation.

Day 12 Prompt: Find a quiet place, sit down, and be still. In what ways was God's presence made known to you today? When are you going to ask him for help? Focus on the present moment.

_____

_____

_____

_____

_____

_____

_____

_____

_____

_____

_____

_____

_____

_____

_____

_____

_____

_____

_____

_____

_____

_____

_____

_____

_____

_____

_____

_____

Your homework:

1. Reread your Day 1 Worry Prayer
2. Give thanks
3. Update your Worry Action Plan
4. Intentionally think and act positively

"The Lord is my light and my salvation —
whom shall I fear?
The Lord is the stronghold of my life —
of **whom shall I be afraid?**"

— Psalm 27:1 (NIV)

DAY 13

Study Scripture

It is important to meditate on God's word daily. Really soak in the scriptures I have provided in this book that precede each day's devotion. Additionally, there are many biblical examples we can learn from as it pertains to worry. Let's look at a few.

Example 1: My favorite worry story is in the book of Mark when the disciples were in the boat with Jesus amid a storm on the Sea of Galilee. The winds and the waves began to pick up. Despite being right next to Jesus, the disciples were still afraid. Their worry caused them to question God's love. Jesus calmed the storm by simply declaring, "Quiet! Be still!" The storm was over—just like that. Jesus asked the disciples, "Why were you afraid when I was with you?"

If you're in the boat with Jesus, you should have your feet kicked up and in your most relaxed state. How are we any different than the disciples in the boat? God is always with us. We can be at ease. Follow the prompting of the Holy Spirit, live in obedience, and magnify his name. Speak life into your storms.

Example 2: The Gospel of Luke tells us a story about Martha who was worrisome and troubled. Jesus was in her home, and her sister Mary sat at the feet of Jesus in awe of him, listening to him speak. Meanwhile, Martha was on edge, wanting everything to be perfectly prepared. The lesson here is to be like Mary and focus on what matters: Jesus. The worry about getting things done is a never-ending list. Focus on what matters in the here and now. Don't make your worries an idol. Martha made organizing and preparation an idol. Make sure God is number one.

Example 3: In the book of Daniel, there were three Hebrew boys—Shadrach, Meshach, and Abednego—and they were placed in the fiery furnace when they refused to bow down to the king's image. Even in the midst of the fire—literally—they were at peace. They were preserved from any harm to their body.

As the biblical examples demonstrate, faith is important to enable us to wait without worry. God truly has our life mapped out and our best interest at heart. Truly meditate on the life of Jesus and how he handled worrisome circumstances. There is so much to be gleaned when we use Jesus as an example.

Day 13 Prompt: What can you learn from the disciples in the boat as it pertains to worry? How about Martha? You can also read about Daniel in the lion's den (Daniel 6:22). What was his level of worry like? How did things play out?

_____
_____
_____
_____
_____
_____
_____
_____
_____
_____
_____
_____
_____
_____
_____
_____
_____
_____
_____
_____
_____
_____

Your homework:

1. Reread your Day 1 Worry Prayer
2. Give thanks
3. Update your Worry Action Plan
4. Intentionally think and act positively

DAY 14

Get Organized

Worry often gets us into a rut, and sometimes it is hard to climb out of it. This rut tends to slow down our productivity. Don't mistake worry for productivity. Getting into action is productivity. Worry in and of itself often does not push us into action to change the circumstance. When things are organized – mentally, physically, and digitally, I find it is easier to get into action and make better decisions.

A clean and organized mental, physical, and digital space can have a very calming effect. If everything has its rightful place, you won't be panicking because you are searching for items. This can take some of the edginess off to solve one problem at a time and prioritize what needs to get done.

Physical: Take time to get rid of or donate items that are unnecessary and cluttering your space. If you haven't used an item for a long time, or you've totally lost sight that it exists, get rid of it. It probably is not a need.

Digital: Scale down the number of email addresses you have and delete the abundance of emails sitting in your inbox. Unsubscribe to unnecessary junk email.

Mental: Organize ideas and areas of your life into electronic files like Dropbox or Google Drive.

Write out your endless to-do list into a checklist form. I find using a checklist is almost like following a very thorough script and my worry and anxiety decreases. There is research about the psychological boost of literally crossing items off a to-do list. Get the most pressing things done, have key conversations, map things out, and get organized. Send the emails, and get the items off your to-do list. God might in fact be waiting on us to get into motion before alleviating some of our worry.

Day 14 Prompt: What do you need to organize mentally, physically, and digitally?

_____

_____

_____

_____

_____

_____

_____

_____

_____

_____

_____

_____

_____

_____

_____

_____

_____

_____

_____

_____

_____

_____

_____

_____

_____

Your homework:

1. Reread your Day 1 Worry Prayer
2. Give thanks
3. Update your Worry Action Plan
4. Intentionally think and act positively

DAY 15

Laugh Regularly

Perhaps we take life too seriously sometimes. Don't get me wrong, life can be serious, but if there is no blood and someone isn't dying, it's often not as serious as we make it out to be. In the moment, it certainly doesn't feel that way.

Consider watching comedies and stand-up shows. Consider even improving your own humor. Find a reason to laugh every day. It will shift your mind away from your worries, even if just temporarily.

When we think back to some of the things we worried about that ended up working out, some of it is truly comical. Before my son was born, I worried and shed actual tears because I didn't know how to use a car seat properly. What made me think I couldn't learn simply by watching a YouTube clip? I've worried how I could survive many situations, and although very challenging, I'm still standing. Try to find an ounce of humor in your everyday situations.

Day 15 Prompt: What was something you genuinely laughed about today? What is something you worried about that worked out and you can actually find humor in it now? What are ways you can lighten the burden of worry and find humor in your situation or everyday life?

_____

_____

_____

_____

_____

_____

_____

_____

_____

_____

_____

_____

_____

_____

_____

_____

_____

_____

_____

_____

_____

_____

_____

_____

Your homework:

1. Reread your Day 1 Worry Prayer
2. Give thanks
3. Update your Worry Action Plan
4. Intentionally think and act positively

"Therefore **do not worry about tomorrow**, for tomorrow will worry about itself. Each day has enough trouble of its own."

— Matthew 6:34 (NIV)

DAY 16

Visualization and Positive Mental Images

What are some key life memories that bring a smile to your face? Put the photos up, create a video photo collage and watch it daily. You can create a vision board or timeline. Try to be intentionally positive with the images in your mind. Allow yourself to view these images often. You have to overpower the negative mental movie reel with a more positive one.

Have a go-to arsenal of mental images that will instantly pull you out of your worry and cause you to remember your blessings. If you are stuck with what to imagine, an image of the laughing Buddha tends to make me at least smile.

1. The "funny" mental image

Example: A child laughing or doing something very silly.

2. The "I'm blessed" mental image

Example: Your closest loved ones.

3. The "big picture/my purpose" mental image

Example: An image of you operating in your purpose/calling, such as an aerial view of you looking at who you impact or what is impacted by your contribution.

4. The "life is sacred" mental image

Example: An image of a loved one who is deceased.

5. The "other side of the scenario" mental image

Example: If your family isn't getting along, think of a time everyone did get along beautifully.

6. The "pivot to something light" mental image

Example: An image of something light and easy, such as enjoying cartoons with a child.

Day 16 Prompt 1: What are some key happy life moments? How can you keep these mental images front and center? How can you reframe an otherwise negative situation to have a positive mental image?

_____

_____

_____

_____

_____

_____

_____

_____

_____

_____

_____

_____

_____

_____

_____

_____

_____

_____

_____

_____

_____

_____

_____

_____

_____

_____

_____

_____

_____

_____

_____

_____

_____

_____

Day 16 Prompt 2: Write out, sketch, or include pictures below of your happy, positive mental images.

The "funny" mental image	The "I'm blessed" mental image
The "big picture/my purpose" mental image	The "life is sacred" mental image
The "other side of the scenario" mental image	The "pivot to something light" mental image

Your homework:

1. Reread your Day 1 Worry Prayer
2. Give thanks
3. Update your Worry Action Plan
4. Intentionally think and act positively

"And we know that in all things **God works for the good of those who love him**, who have been called according to his purpose."

— Romans 8:28 (NIV)

DAY 17

Share the Responsibility

Life can be hard sometimes, but don't feel the need to be the person who has to complete every task or the entire project. Things will get accomplished even if you don't complete the task. If a project is intended to be a group effort, do your portion well and don't give yourself the added responsibility of taking on more unless the Holy Spirit directs you to do so. Stay in your lane. Tend to your assigned portion. Not everything is intended for you to do. Perform your task, especially as it aligns to your strengths, and let others have a role.

Make more things in life a team effort. Team success always feels great. In my experience, the result of a dynamic team effort has always resulted in a better outcome than if it had been done alone. Sometimes we rob people of life experience when we take on too much of the responsibility.

If you are the person in charge, release some of the responsibility and delegate. When we think everything has to be on us, that is the worry–pride connection. We don't have to be the be-all and do-all. We were never intended to carry the weight of the world alone. Sometimes you have to do your part and then step out of the way to allow God—through the work of others—to do his part.

Day 17 Prompt: Do you always tend to take on more burdens when in a group dynamic? How can you release control? What are your strengths? What are your weaknesses? Can you delegate to someone else?

_____

_____

_____

_____

_____

_____

_____

_____

_____

_____

_____

_____

_____

_____

_____

_____

_____

_____

_____

_____

_____

_____

_____

Your homework:

1. Reread your Day 1 Worry Prayer
2. Give thanks
3. Update your Worry Action Plan
4. Intentionally think and act positively

"**Trust in the Lord with all your heart**
and lean not on your own understanding;
in all your ways submit to him,
and he will make your paths straight."

— Proverbs 3:5–6 (NIV)

DAY 18

Move Forward Quickly When Disappointed

Life happens, and it has many disappointing moments with people and situations. It is sometimes a blow to your self-confidence. Worry coupled with disappointment is a heavy combination. It is hard not to personalize disappointment, but don't go down that road. Face it and lean into it, but don't stay there too long. Take a break. Find a place to quickly process and mentally place disappointment, almost like a mental disappointment box. Take small steps and release your attachment. Detach from the outcome and find gratitude in the journey. Refocus.

There have been opportunities where God distinctly told me to pursue something, but I didn't get a "yes" or acceptance. I would ask, "But, God, you set up the conditions for me to be the perfect candidate. Why God?"

Disappointment can often leave us frozen and no longer willing to try, hope, believe, or plan. Time often reveals God's master design. There is a saying, "When God closes a door, he opens a window." No preparation is ever in vain. Disappointment is often one of our greatest teachers and can serve as a means to pivot us in the right direction. Thank God for the lessons in the trying. What are the positive aspects to disappointment? What is the silver lining? Perhaps preparing for the job you didn't get, is a set up for a future job acceptance. Where God ultimately placed me has always proven to be where I was supposed to be and when I was supposed to be there. He might place you somewhere for healing, so that when you are fully prepared for the promotion, you are ready and fully healed. One of the sweetest parts of being disappointed in a situation is the later revelation as to why God did what he did. The dots all really do connect one day.

If it is disappointment in a person, consciously recall positive memories with the person. Don't allow disappointment to define your identity or anyone else's. Then move forward from disappointment since this seems to keep us stuck and only amplifies the worry. There is that infamous phrase, "It is what it is." We can't get too hung up with what went wrong or who let us down. It is already done. Move forward. Moving forward might mean without them. People and circumstances are very complicated. We are all learning and growing, and in different places on the continuum. Give others tons and tons of grace. We can't get too stuck in these dark emotions.

Get better at bouncing back or rebounding. You might need some time and space. Learn from it. Apologize. Accept the apology. If the apology never comes, have a conversation and/or decide if you will move forward with them or without them. Just don't live there. Monitor your emotional investment in certain people and situations.

I have a hunch that God allows certain disappointments so that he can step in or use others to be a miracle in a situation, or maybe to delay the timing of certain events to ensure things work in your favor. I believe he also allows disappointment for growth opportunities. What I also enjoy about disappointment is God often sends small victories and positive people and situations to remind us, "You might be disappointed right now, but remember I work all things together for good."

Read the following poems:

Discouragement

> Discouragement
> Is set up to wear you down
> To cut off spiritual vitality
> A satanic attempt to

Sever your joy
The internal fire within
Don't fall for it

Perceived Closed Doors

Disappointment could be God saying,
"Not now, but later, under different conditions
You won't thrive in this space . . .
I have another assignment
Better aligned to your strengths."

Disappointment could be God saying,
"I want you to build with someone else
I want you to see how you should NOT conduct yourself
Pivot your focus
Right now, I want you to enjoy life more . . .
This will pull you away from the bounty of life
You have outgrown that space."

Disappointment is often God saying, "I have something much better in store. Something will come out of this. Trust me." Thank you, God, for perceived closed doors.

Day 18 Prompt: Have you been weighed down with disappointment? How can you compartmentalize this disappointment and shift your energy to a more hopeful and optimistic place? Consider a person or situation you are currently disappointed in, and then think of 3 positive memories. Write those memories down. Following those memories, write, "I just can't throw away this relationship because I am currently disappointed." Then decide what you will do from there.

_____

_____

_____

_____

_____

_____

_____

_____

_____

_____

_____

_____

_____

_____

_____

_____

_____

_____

_____

_____

Your homework:

1. Reread your Day 1 Worry Prayer
2. Give thanks
3. Update your Worry Action Plan
4. Intentionally think and act positively

"Do not be anxious about anything, but in every situation, by prayer and petition, with thanksgiving, **present your requests to God**."

— Philippians 4:6 (NIV)

"Nebuchadnezzar then approached the opening of the blazing furnace and shouted, 'Shadrach, Meshach and Abednego, servants of the Most High God, come out! Come here!' So Shadrach, Meshach and Abednego came out of the fire, and the satraps, prefects, governors and royal advisers crowded around them. They saw that **the fire had not harmed their bodies**, nor was a hair of their heads singed; their robes were not scorched, and there was no smell of fire on them."

— Daniel 3:26–27 (NIV)

DAY 19

Work through Devastation

Like the disciples in the boat with Jesus, they believed the strong winds would destroy them. No matter the worst-case scenario, who said it would be the end for you? People heal and situations can be restored. Miracles happen all around us. Whatever you are worried about won't have the final say. God has the final say. God will get you through any worrisome moment or season. What doesn't kill you certainly makes you stronger. One day it will all make sense. Perhaps the strong winds on the boat were a way to teach the disciples faith. We have to remember that God is there and with us, even in our most challenging moments. He won't let this situation wipe you out or take you under. He will rescue you or be in the circumstance with you.

Day 19 Prompt: No matter the outcome of the thing you're worried about, do you think you will survive? Reflect on a time you healed or rebounded from a setback. Do you think you could do it again? What did you do as it pertained to trust and faith that got you through?

_____

_____

_____

_____

_____

_____

_____

_____

_____

_____

_____

_____

_____

_____

_____

_____

_____

_____

_____

_____

_____

_____

_____

Your homework:

1. Reread your Day 1 Worry Prayer
2. Give thanks
3. Update your Worry Action Plan
4. Intentionally think and act positively

"I am unworthy of **all the kindness and faithfulness you have shown** your servant . . ."

— Genesis 32:10 (NIV)

DAY 20

God Has a Master Plan

Consider God's past faithfulness through answered prayer. Has he ever left you before? Our present worry often keeps us so fixated that we forget God's past faithfulness. God continuously does amazing things. You have probably been sick and gotten well. You probably had various personal and professional goals that you have attained. You have probably had to pray your way out of the pit of despair on more than one occasion, but you are still standing.

What amazes me is God's track record. I have been in what I perceived to be impossible situations, and to see God move on my behalf has been astounding and quite humbling. I've been in situations where I felt God may have forgotten about me, and years later he did something amazing to show me there is a grand plan for my life. We make plans and endless to-do lists, and God has a keen way of rearranging our plans for our ultimate benefit.

You may have even hit rock bottom. And even at rock bottom, God extended his grace and mercy. You may encounter situations that feel like scarcity and lack when in fact God is teaching you discipline and focus. Miraculously God turns our situations around for our good. If we take the time to reflect on our experiences, we become wiser through each and every situation that comes our way.

Day 20 Prompt: Recall God's track record. What are some past answered prayers?

_____

_____

_____

_____

_____

_____

_____

_____

_____

_____

_____

_____

_____

_____

_____

_____

_____

_____

_____

_____

_____

_____

_____

_____

Your homework:

1. Reread your Day 1 Worry Prayer
2. Give thanks
3. Update your Worry Action Plan
4. Intentionally think and act positively

"Come to me, all you who are weary and burdened, and **I will give you rest.**"

— Matthew 11:28 (NIV)

DAY 21

Be Prepared

Preparation and Skill Building

Preparation often helps to reduce worry. If you are going to give a presentation, you want to have your speaking points lined up. Some people can wing it, but a lot of people can't or at least don't do it well. If you are worried about landing a job, preparing for the interview helps. Whatever your level of expertise, keep refining your skill set and improving, and the same can be said of your weaknesses. Try to improve in these areas. For example, if money makes you worried, take a few budgeting and finance classes and apply the skills that were taught. Create a budget and practice mindful spending. If something happening to you or your loved one makes you worried, take the steps to get arrangements in order.

Social Anxiety

Being prepared is half the battle. Next, when you are most worrisome, "Fake it till you make it." Many are concerned about how they will be perceived and what people will think about them. Prepare for these moments as well. For instance, come up with two or three stories you can share and the questions you can ask others. Pretend you are your most brave and composed self. Let the feelings wash away like water. Use your imagination. If you are more worried around certain people, pretend they are your best friend and engage with them as you would your best friend. Be prepared, rehearse, tighten things up, and have a backup plan.

93

Day 21 Prompt: What future moments make you worried? What is your level of preparation usually like? Consider an aspect of your life that makes you nervous. Would preparation alleviate some of your worry? Are there situations you can pretend your way through for the time being until you build up your confidence?

_____

_____

_____

_____

_____

_____

_____

_____

_____

_____

_____

_____

_____

_____

_____

_____

_____

_____

_____

_____

_____

_____

_____

Your homework:

1.   Reread your Day 1 Worry Prayer
2.   Give thanks
3.   Update your Worry Action Plan
4.   Intentionally think and act positively

"The weapons we fight with are not the weapons of the world. On the contrary, they have divine power to **demolish strongholds**. We demolish arguments and every pretension that sets itself up against the knowledge of God, and we take captive every thought to make it obedient to Christ."

— 2 Corinthians 10:4–5 (NIV)

Whoever dwells in the shelter of the Most High
will **rest in the shadow of the Almighty**.
I will say of the Lord, "He is my refuge and my fortress,
my God, in whom I trust."
Surely he will save you
from the fowler's snare
and from the deadly pestilence.
He will cover you with his feathers,
and under his wings you will find refuge;
his faithfulness will be your shield and rampart.
You will not fear the terror of night,
nor the arrow that flies by day,
nor the pestilence that stalks in the darkness,
nor the plague that destroys at midday.
A thousand may fall at your side,
ten thousand at your right hand,
but it will not come near you.
You will only observe with your eyes
and see the punishment of the wicked.
If you say, "The Lord is my refuge,"
and you make the Most High your dwelling,
no harm will overtake you,
no disaster will come near your tent.
For he will command his angels concerning you
to guard you in all your ways;
they will lift you up in their hands,
so that you will not strike your foot against a stone.
You will tread on the lion and the cobra;

you will trample the great lion and the serpent.
"Because he loves me," says the Lord, "I will rescue him;
I will protect him, for he acknowledges my name.
He will call on me, and I will answer him;
I will be with him in trouble,
I will deliver him and honor him.
With long life I will satisfy him
and show him my salvation."

— Psalm 91 (NIV)

DAY 22

Don't Let the Enemy Win

Sometimes your worry increases because it is in fact spiritual warfare. The enemy stirs up your worries to get you discouraged and defeated. This could happen if you are doing something for the glory of God. If you are finally breaking that addiction, finally stepping up as a noble parent, finally committing your life to God, the devil will not be too thrilled. Warfare often brings forth feelings of being overwhelmed, distracted, and in chaos. Warfare means it's time to pause and be still, move toward peace (see Day 7), pray and ask God for direction, then just watch him work. Also, whatever you don't heal serves as an easy access point for the devil. Proclaim, "God, take this worry away! Heal my wounds so that the devil can have limited access to me. Please fight my battles, God." Pray, fast, read his word, praise, worship, obey. Forgive, give, be humble, and patient. Have faith, endure, do good, and live with purpose. The attack is temporary. There is an end date.

God might be waiting for you to make a key move, remove a particular stronghold, get more disciplined in your diet or finances, reach out to someone to express forgiveness, or visit a family member who needs you before the worry subsides and perhaps the problem is resolved.

Never forget who God is. He is known to be the God of the reversal. What you see now might not be what you see in due time. Be strong and steadfast. Have him fight this battle with you and for you. Give him all the glory when the battle ends.

Don't be afraid of the opposition and be sure to do what God has called you to do. You can't be successful and be afraid of people. They will always run you away from fulfilling God's call on your life.

21 Warfare Strategies:

1. Increase your faith
2. Fast and pray
3. Read the Bible and recall God's promises
4. Praise and worship
5. Follow the prompting of the Holy Spirit and obey
6. Forgive
7. Pay tithes
8. Give an offering
9. Be humble
10. Connect with other believers
11. Love
12. Be grateful
13. Be patient
14. Be aware of division and isolation in the atmosphere
15. Bounce back from disappointment
16. Rest and be silent at key moments
17. Do good
18. Stay focused
19. Exude joy
20. Remember your purpose
21. Be strong in the Lord and endure

Day 22 Prompt: Are you enduring a spiritual attack? What is your battle plan? How can you reduce your worry during this season of warfare? Have you asked God for help?

_____

_____

_____

_____

_____

_____

_____

_____

_____

_____

_____

_____

_____

_____

_____

_____

_____

_____

_____

_____

_____

_____

_____

Your homework:

1. Reread your Day 1 Worry Prayer
2. Give thanks
3. Update your Worry Action Plan
4. Intentionally think and act positively

"Let us not become weary in doing good, for at the proper time we will reap a harvest if we do not give up."

— Galatians 6:9 (NIV)

DAY 23

Heal Old Wounds

People are often not in a heightened state of worry because of their own choosing. We are all doing what we know. Many of our insecurities that cause us to be worried are connected to wounds, traumas, and various occurrences from the past. Do the work under God's guidance to try to heal. Use your past for purpose. Explore tools that will allow you to push through when the unhealed scars resurface. For example, if you lived in a home with food scarcity, you might have a gluttonous side to you because you may, subconsciously, still be worried that food won't be available. Even though you may now have ample food, your mind has become programmed to worry about having enough. It's interesting how our minds hold onto negative experiences.

Insecurities, weaknesses, and vulnerabilities are how the enemy easily accesses many of us. Even the most confident person has old wounds and triggers. Accept the fact we all have strengths and weaknesses. Identify your strengths, and work on improving your weaknesses. Don't judge someone else for their weaknesses. Steer far away from the comparisons, categories, groupings, and rankings. Work though all the things that seem to trigger a response in your body.

Do the work to try to reduce those feelings of insecurity. It might be a combination of various therapies. Work on developing some go-to strategies to de-escalate yourself when wound up after being triggered. Rally in support to stabilize and get to baseline. Be open to receive support.

Level up, elevate, and build yourself up in a safe, secure, and regulated environment. Find a safe community that will affirm and support you as you do the work to improve your life. Set goals, but more importantly, plan for bold moves to really push you forward. Put yourself in the right spaces to build your confidence.

Start believing in yourself. Build your confidence in your area of worry. Study, watch videos, listen to audiobooks and podcasts, take courses, or talk to a professional. Put in the work to try to grow and improve.

How else can you work on insecurity? Get to know God and become secure in him.

Day 23 Prompt 1: What old wounds does the enemy access to get you wound up and worrisome? What are your triggers? What can you do at the height of those feelings? Jot them down below.

	Triggers (often from the past)	Worry, feeling, or emotion that pops up	De-escalation strategy, reassurance tool
1			
2			
3			
4			
5			

<u>Day 23 Prompt 2:</u> "I am Mantra."

Say all of the following three times. Create your own "I Am" mantra if you would like.

I am loved.
I am loving.
I am kind.
I am growing.
I am maturing.
I am evolving.
I am happy.
I am healthy.
I am content.
I am powerful.
I am strong.
I am confident.
I am worthy.
I am enough.

Your homework:

1. Reread your Day 1 Worry Prayer
2. Give thanks
3. Update your Worry Action Plan
4. Intentionally think and act positively

"You shall have **no other Gods before me**."

— Exodus 20:3 (NIV)

DAY 24

Don't Idolize Your Worry

God has to be number one, not your worry. He has the power to control and change a circumstance.

Worry can quickly become idolizing. We can spend so much time worrying, then try to fix someone or something, that we grow weary and at our wits' end. We evaluate it, analyze it, and judge it to exhaustion. Our relationships also tend to suffer because of our worry.

In *Waiting Well: A 21-day Writing Journey to Increase Patience*, I discuss making idols out of our wants and desires.

"When you want something badly, you tend to have tunnel vision. That's all you focus on. You tend not to look up and around to see the blessings in front of you. Idolizing the acquisition of the thing, whatever it is, will consume your life. You will not take as much notice of the small blessings throughout the day, or how you are truly already blessed in a major way."

If your worry is more of a focal point in your life than loving others, serving others, and praising God, then your priorities might be out of order. Here are some key priority and focus areas:

1. God
2. Spouse
3. Child (academic, social-emotional development, goals)
4. Parents
5. Siblings

6. Health
7. Finances
8. Purpose
9. Key relationships
10. Connection to various communities (school, church)
11. Job/occupation
12. Care of living space

Consider how you can redistribute your thoughts to other areas of your life that need your attention.

<u>Day 24 Prompt:</u> Think about your distribution of attention and focus. Who or what has received more of your mental focus? What areas of your life have been untended or neglected due to your worry in a certain area of your life?

_____

Your homework:

1. Reread your Day 1 Worry Prayer
2. Give thanks
3. Update your Worry Action Plan
4. Intentionally think and act positively

"In their hearts humans plan their course,
but **the Lord establishes their steps**."

— Proverbs 16:9 (NIV)

DAY 25

Trust the Process and God's Timing

Give situations time. Nothing is as definitive as it appears to be. God is moving. Change is happening during the waiting, even in what appears to be silence and not hearing from God. We worry when we assume progress isn't being made, things will never restore, or things will never improve. God reverses situations. God restores things that were lost. God heals. The key is that you are learning and growing.

Success is best when it doesn't come overnight. You will then be able to handle it with much better care. If you are worrying about when you will have relief or attain something, let your request be known and actively move toward it and listen for God's direction. He might tell you to suppress the urge and idolization of the thing until further notice.

I remember worrying about many things that I still have documented in my journals. Most of the things I worried would happen actually never came to pass. Then there are many unfavorable things that have happened over the years that I could have never fathomed. My worries did not align to my reality. Let me say that again: *MY WORRIES DID NOT ALIGN TO MY REALITY.* What I worried about never happened, but what actually did wind up happening was something I never could have imagined. In other words, our worry predictions are usually off.

Now that I am more attuned to the complexities of family, marriage, parenting, managing health, finances, relationships, and a career, I'm so glad God scaffolded life for me. It would have been a catastrophe if all of my desires happened when and how I wanted them to, and at a rapid speed. Filled with highs and lows, the pacing was perfect for my personal growth and development.

The Circle of Divine Elevation

Focus on the following: prayer, giving things time, moments of action, moments of silence and reflection, and a continuous growth mindset. The silent reflection is a critical time to soak things in, reflect, process, and extract lessons. This is also a time to assess progress and your own feelings. How do you feel? What progress is being made? We tend to continuously push ahead with the doing and taking in more and more, but we rarely take the time to rest and consider ways to apply the lessons from experience. When you can honor times of action and inaction under the direction of God, you will continuously level up and elevate in mind and spirit.

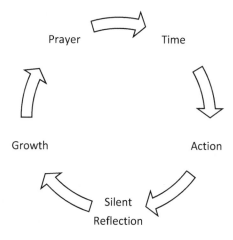

Day 25 Prompt: Reflect on the Circle of Divine Elevation. Consider the cycle of prayer, giving things time, moments of action, moments of silence and reflection, and a continuous growth mindset. What comes to mind? Reflect on a situation in your life that God slowly built you up through these phases. What was revealed to you?

_____
_____
_____
_____
_____
_____
_____
_____
_____
_____
_____
_____
_____
_____
_____
_____
_____
_____
_____
_____
_____
_____
_____

Your homework:

1. Reread your Day 1 Worry Prayer
2. Give thanks
3. Update your Worry Action Plan
4. Intentionally think and act positively

"For **we are God's handiwork**, created in Christ Jesus to do good works, which God prepared in advance for us to do."

— Ephesians 2:10 (NIV)

DAY 26

Your Life's Purpose

Remembering to operate out of purpose and God's call for your life helps you to lift higher and out of worrisome situations. It is often our area of giftedness and purpose that come under attack. Purpose can get us back on track. Bringing your gifts to a circumstance can help you shift from worry to meaning and purpose.

We have specific gifts that are to be used to glorify God's name. This is our light. If we know God has us in a situation to use our gifts, we know God will take care of us in that situation. Press forward in using that gift and see what happens. It won't be easy, but kingdom work never is.

When we focus less on what is making us anxious and instead on our purpose or how we can bring light in that dark situation, the hardship holds less power. We must focus on God's purpose for our lives and shine our light ever so brightly.

Day 26 Prompt: What is your purpose? In what areas do you find the most meaning in your life? How could you use this knowing to pull yourself out of worry?

_____

_____

_____

_____

_____

_____

_____

_____

_____

_____

_____

_____

_____

_____

_____

_____

_____

_____

_____

_____

_____

_____

Your homework:

1. Reread your Day 1 Worry Prayer
2. Give thanks
3. Update your Worry Action Plan
4. Intentionally think and act positively

Sheryl Walker

"God is our **refuge and strength**,
an ever-present help in trouble."

— Psalm 46:1 (NIV)

DAY 27

Be Reasonable and Rational

One of the many problems with worry is it can leave us frozen and unable to think straight. If we are too focused on our worry, we can make poor decisions. But you've got this! Get to a quiet space, pray, and ask God to help you to think clearly. Look at what is in front of you. If you are worried about an outcome, list the pros and cons. Think, "At this point, what can I do?" Make a decision under God's direction, then put one foot in front of the other and move forward, and your pace will eventually pick up. Just getting into gear can have a domino effect and other important things can get done. Turn things over to God while taking the God ordained steps you can take. You are surrendering, while also remaining obedient and attuned to God's direction. Become stronger and more powerful than the worry. The power lives within you through the power of God. Read the Serenity Prayer below three times.

Serenity Prayer

> God, grant me the serenity
> to accept the things I cannot change,
> the courage to change the things I can,
> and the wisdom to know the difference.
> Living one day at a time,
> enjoying one moment at a time;
> accepting hardship as a pathway to peace;

117

taking, as Jesus did,
this sinful world as it is,
not as I would have it;
trusting that You will make all things right
if I surrender to Your will;
so that I may be reasonably happy in this life
and supremely happy with You forever in the next.

Amen.

— Reinhold Niebuhr

Day 27 Prompt: Consider your top worry. Decide courses of action to alleviate this worry. Create a list of pros and cons for each course of action. Get into gear.

_____
_____
_____
_____
_____
_____
_____
_____
_____
_____
_____
_____
_____
_____
_____
_____
_____
_____
_____
_____
_____
_____
_____
_____

Your homework:

1. Reread your Day 1 Worry Prayer
2. Give thanks
3. Update your Worry Action Plan
4. Intentionally think and act positively

"Do not conform to the pattern of this world, but **be transformed by the renewing of your mind**. Then you will be able to test and approve what God's will is—his good, pleasing and perfect will."

— Romans 12:2 (NIV)

"Finally, brothers and sisters, whatever is true, whatever is noble, whatever is right, whatever is pure, whatever is lovely, whatever is admirable—**if anything is excellent or praiseworthy—think about such things**."

— Philippians 4:8 (NIV)

DAY 28

Work Toward Mental Freedom

Captivity is in your mind. The goal is mental freedom. This is the most liberating act. You can be imprisoned figuratively and literally but can be mentally free. Worrying is not freedom. It is bondage. It is a mental prison. Worry takes your mind as a hostage. This is not biblical thinking. It is not a loving place to be.

You can be in an unfavorable situation and decide how you will operate in that situation. Some of your actions and allowing your mind to stay in the pit of worry contribute to remaining in mental bondage. Bondage is exacerbated when our diet is poor, we overdo things, are out of balance, don't work toward healing our wounds, and sow seeds of division, criticism, and conflict. When we are out of balance, we don't allow ourselves to have appropriate boundaries, and our worries will naturally increase.

On the contrary, when we work on expansion, maintaining and nurturing healthy relationships, commit to healing, make smart decisions to ensure the wellbeing of our families, work together to share resources and knowledge, build each other up to be fully whole, and have appropriate boundaries in our relationship with others, we have set up the conditions for less worry.

See the beauty in imperfection. Imperfection adds color to life. So much of our anxiety comes from trying to be perfect. Give yourself lots and lots of grace.

We have more control of our mental freedom than we are allowing.

Consider what you really need. What is at the heart of your worries? Is it a need for security? Validation? Meaning? Intimacy? Progress?

The Mind

What do we allow to take root, in our mind?
Let it grow
Let it fester
Grow arms
And legs
And a complete body
Imagination growing rampant
Wild
Weeds out of control
Movie reel of the past
On repeat
The fear of the future
Has us creating all
The possible paths
And going down each
And every one of them
Never present
Always back there or over there
Never here
Enjoying the melodic tunes of music
The artistry and genius
Of the lyrics
Laughing at the joke
She just told
Smiling at the baby
Who just invited you into their world
Did you even catch that?
Commit to freeing the mind of worry. It is truly an act of self-love.

Day 28 Prompt: In what ways are you bound by worry? What does it prevent you from doing? What behaviors hold you in bondage or captivity? What behaviors do you need to adopt that demonstrate freedom?

_____

_____

_____

_____

_____

_____

_____

_____

_____

_____

_____

_____

_____

_____

_____

_____

_____

_____

_____

_____

_____

_____

_____

_____

_____

_____

Your homework:

1. Reread your Day 1 Worry Prayer
2. Give thanks
3. Update your Worry Action Plan
4. Intentionally think and act positively

"Blessed is the man who **trusts in the Lord**, and whose hope is the Lord. For he shall be like a tree planted by the waters, which spreads out its roots by the river, and will not fear when heat comes; but its leaf will be green, and will not be anxious in the year of drought, nor will cease from yielding fruit."

— Jeremiah 17:7–8 (New King James Version)

DAY 29

Surrender

One of my first steps when worry begins to rise is to be still, move toward peace, and talk to God.

My entire twenties were a constant state of worry. Perhaps some of my angst could have been ambition; however, my degree of worry was incessant. Would I be hired? When would I move out? Would I find the right apartment? Would I check off all the categories on life's checklist? I never could get settled on the notion that the "how" was God's job.

After going though plenty of heartache and pain, I got to a point where I could say, "Thank you, God, for revealing those important lessons to me during life's challenges." The key aspect is to heal, extract the lessons, and try not to repeat the same mistakes.

Your present circumstances don't dictate how it will always be. "This too shall pass." Things will change, and that's for certain.

As we wait, we need to wait well. Life sometimes requires a whole lot of patience. Never rush God. While we often want relief, numbing out with drugs or anything else isn't the best option. It can lead to great loss and much more.

I can't help but to think of Noah. Even though God told Noah to build the ark, the storm and the wait caused Noah to worry. God did eventually calm the storm. Always remember the story of Noah. Remember God's past track record. He will be with you. He will protect you. He will always provide for you. When worry ebbs and flows, like the waves in a storm, say, "God, help me with my feelings of worry. Please step in and help me.

Send a host of angels to help me to calm my spirit. Please take care of all my needs. I need you." God will meet your needs.

It wasn't until my thirties that I had been through enough tumultuous seasons that I discovered surrendering to God was the best and only thing I could do. Surrendering always precedes a major move of God. It is worth repeating: *Surrendering always precedes a major move of God.* Truly turning 100 percent of the situation over to God. Worry would never get me anywhere. I began to learn how to quiet some of the extraneous noises of life, such as people's behavior and opinions, and begin to zero in on God to get me through any and all circumstances. Worry will push you into a cave, and it will take a lot for you to come out.

Truly remove your hands from the steering wheel of life. Have good intentions. Do everything with care and God will see your heart. Make your requests known. After turning it over to him, be at peace. God LOVES stepping in. He loves to intervene. Ask God for a supernatural miracle: "Lord, I don't know how you are going to do it, but I believe you will do it." Then move over and let God do what he does best: work all things out for our good, even our worries. When God responds, don't ignore his feedback or discipline. What makes you worrisome in one area might force you to be extra vigilant in another. He is truly the captain of our lives. Let go and let God take charge.

You could be so close to a breakthrough. Start believing God for miracles. Our God is the same God that parted the Red Sea. What's beautiful about miracles is that sometimes they come along and you didn't even realize you needed that particular miracle. God is really the best!

Day 29 Prompt: Write down the miracle(s) in your life that you are believing God will manifest for you.

Miracle 1:

Miracle 2:

Miracle 3:

Miracle 4:

Miracle 5:

Miracle 6:

Your homework:

1. Reread your Day 1 Worry Prayer
2. Give thanks
3. Update your Worry Action Plan
4. Intentionally think and act positively

"I keep my eyes always on the Lord.
With him at my right hand, I will not be shaken."

— Psalm 16:8 (NIV)

DAY 30

Worry Management Is Ongoing Work

I wish things were as simple as officially putting an end to worry and then moving on. Worry seems to ebb and flow through many seasons of our lives.

We can't make worry our daily narrative or our immediate coping mechanism. When will we ever allow God to live up to his reputation?

The ability to release our worries to God is ongoing work. To choose prayer over worry requires building a whole new set of go-to coping mechanisms, and many of us are not necessarily ready to release what we know is comfortable. But where is worry taking us? Today let's commit to a new approach.

Take things one step at a time. Build in periods of rest and reflection to process and apply all you are discovering about yourself and building your trust in God.

You are going to be all right. It gets better. Be patient with yourself. The only unchanging aspect of life is God. He is our rock. He is our anchor.

Day 30 Prompt: Are you willing to continue the worry-free journey? How will you ensure you continue this ongoing work? What strategies will you develop into a habit?

_____

_____

_____

_____

_____

_____

_____

_____

_____

_____

_____

_____

_____

_____

_____

_____

_____

_____

_____

_____

_____

_____

_____

Your homework:

1. Reread your Day 1 Worry Prayer
2. Give thanks
3. Update your Worry Action Plan
4. Intentionally think and act positively

Bonus Section

Parenting

For many parents, our children are a primary source of worry. Parents are responsible for caring and raising children while taking measures to prevent them from harm. It sometimes feels like worrying and parenting go hand in hand. However, I do know that God will protect my children just like he protects me. We must trust God. Whatever our children have experienced and will experience can be used for their purpose. It's almost impossible to micromanage their lives, especially their adult lives. The truth is, we can't be with them every single moment of the day. We can try our absolute best to pray over them and set up the conditions to mitigate harm, and let God do the rest.

5 Ps for Parenting with Less Worry:

1. **Pray**: Hand control over to God. Pray before conception and throughout their entire lives.
2. **Pay Attention**: Minimize distractions. What does your child need? Most often it is your time and outward expression of love.
3. **Preventative Measures**: What can you have in place to prevent some of the unfavorable things from happening? When exposed to certain facets of life, be sure to explain.
4. **Proactive Measures**: When something does present itself, how should you respond? Early intervention is ideal. Again, expose and explain.
5. **Patience**: Have patience for things to improve. For your child to evolve. For you to evolve as a parent. To feel a sense of true mutual forgiveness and/or acceptance.

Bonus Section Prompt: If applicable, how has God demonstrated his love and care as it pertains to your children? What worries do you need to surrender to God as it pertains to your children?

_____

_____

_____

_____

_____

_____

_____

_____

_____

_____

_____

_____

_____

_____

_____

_____

_____

_____

_____

_____

_____

_____

_____

Your homework:

1. Reread your Day 1 Worry Prayer
2. Give thanks
3. Update your Worry Action Plan
4. Intentionally think and act positively

CONCLUSION

Thank you for going on this beautiful worry journey. Thank you for being open to growth and allowing yourself to be stretched in a new way.

As I mentioned in the introduction, birds don't worry about their daily sustenance. They trust that they will find their food. After taking this journey, I can't help but to look at birds now through a new lens. Birds are always taken care of. I have to make a daily mental note: "Be like the birds." If today were my last day on Earth, I would want to be as mentally free as a bird.

If we think of our lives as a stack of paper, and each passing day is one less piece of paper in the stack, who wants to waste away life with worry? It's uncomfortable to imagine, but the stack is dwindling.

When we know God, we know worry is the opposite of trust. Worry doesn't know God like we do. We often forget what he has brought us out of. We begin trying to control a world we cannot control. Never forget that you always have direct access to the one who controls it all. Invite God into your worries. He will protect you from any harm and bring you peace. Have faith and trust God, even in the ugliest moments. He will come through right on time, even if it feels like it is just in the nick of time. Ask God to reveal your course of action. Obey him. He has the ultimate authority. The threat is not real.

Always see worry as an opportunity. Perhaps it is warfare or an indication that many of our personal wounds have not healed. This could be an opportunity for God to humble us and apologize or forgive, and to show our dependence on him and release control.

Remember, worry makes us neglect important people or things. What are you neglecting because you are idolizing your worries? What are you missing out on—creativity, peace, being a better parent, a better spouse, a better employee? God's special assignment? Blessings? Miracles? At what point do you pivot into action?

It is much easier said than done. Continue to ask God to calm your worries and to show you the path to mental freedom. I am sending you loads and loads of compassion and grace as you figure things out. May you discover more of God and his peace that surpasses all understanding. And don't forget to laugh and enjoy life in this very moment!

ABOUT THE AUTHOR

Sheryl Walker is an educator and has facilitated 100+ one-on-one adult coaching conversations. Her writing is inspired by her own life journey and those she has coached professionally. Her books are centered around personal growth through the acquisition of new learning, self-reflection, and daily writing. Daily writing has often served as an enlightenment ritual as a way to endure life's most challenging moments. She is also the author of the books *Armored Up: A 30-Day Writing Journey to Combat Spiritual Warfare, More Grateful: A 21-Day Writing Journey to Increase Gratitude, Waiting Well: A 21-Day Writing Journey to Increase Patience, Forgive Anyway: A 30-Day Writing Journey to Total Forgiveness, Love Poems to God,* and *The Black Girls Guide to College Success.* She is one of the co-authors of the book *The Higher-Level Method: Success Stories on How to Master Your Business and Life Goals* by Darlene Williams. She enjoys writing in her leisure.

Printed in the United States
by Baker & Taylor Publisher Services